Planning Basketball Practice

by Sidney Goldstein

author of **The Basketball Coach's Bible**

and **The Basketball Player's Bible**

GOLDEN AURA PUBLISHING
The Nitty-Gritty Basketball Series

Planning Basketball Practice

by Sidney Goldstein

Published by:

GOLDEN AURA PUBLISHING

Post Office Box 41012

Philadelphia, PA 19127 U.S.A.

Second Edition Copyright © 1999 by Sidney Goldstein

Printed in the U.S.A.

2nd Printing Sept. 2000

Library of Congress Catalog Card Number: 94-96496

Goldstein, Sidney

Planning Basketball Practice:

Sidney Goldstein.--Second Edition, 1999

Basketball-Coaching

ISBN 1-884357-09-1

Softcover

Contents

Introduction

Over many years of coaching, planning, and studying, I found ways to teach each and every skill even to the most unskilled player. This scheme of learning did not come from any book. I tried things in practice. I modified them till they worked. Even players who could not simultaneously chew bubble gum and walk learned the skills. This booklet, part of **The Basketball Coach's Bible**, is one result of this effort. I believe you too can benefit from my work.

Who Can Use This Information

This booklet is the perfect tool for anybody who wants to coach, teach, and/or learn basketball:

- A parent who wants to teach his or her child
- A player who wants to understand the game better
- A little league or recreation league coach
- A high school or junior high school coach
- A college coach, a professional coach
- A women's or a men's coach

This booklet contains material from **The Basketball Coach's Bible**. Chapters 1 and 2 explain how to plan–the key to coaching–and teach at practice. Highlights include the Practice Planning Guide that helps incorporate all the skills into each practice and a list of Do Nots that points out many ineffective ideas and methods. Chapter 3 presents strategies for picking a team, dealing with referees, playing on unfamiliar courts, and more. Chapters 4-6 present a warm down, how to keep shot and game statistics, sample practices, and blank planning and other forms for your use.

Because there are so many references to the lessons in **The Basketball Coach's Bible,** the Coach's Table of Lessons follows as Chapter 7. You can see how the many planning features look together in action in Lesson 8.1 from **The Basketball Coach's Bible**, Chapter 8.

The references from **The Basketball Coach's Bible** are not needed to understand this material. However, they are helpful to those who want more detail and/or plan to study the larger book.

The phrase "Warm Down" that is used throughout the text might better be described as a "Cool Down". The Cool Down demonstrated in Video 3, Planning Basketball Practice I, thought different than this one, achieves the same goals.

Golden Aura's Nitty-Gritty Basketball Series
by Sidney Goldstein

See the description in the back of this book.

The Basketball Coach's Bible

The Basketball Player's Bible

The Basketball Shooting Guide

The Basketball Scoring Guide

The Basketball Dribbling Guide

The Basketball Defense Guide

The Basketball Pass Cut Catch Guide

Basketball Fundamentals

Planning Basketball Practice

Videos for the Guides soon available

HOW TO CONTACT THE AUTHOR

The author seeks your comments about this book. Sidney Goldstein is available for consultation and clinics with coaches and players. Contact him at:

Golden Aura Publishing
PO Box 41012
Philadelphia, PA 19127
215 438-4459

Chapter One

1

Practice Planning

Planning is the key to teaching and learning. Plan for the season as well as for daily practices. The lessons and the guide below assist in making everyday plans. Seasonal planning depends on an evaluation of your players' ability; this evaluation determines both the number of lessons taught and how much time is spent on each. I caution you not to skip lessons. Consider spending less time on lessons your players execute well or combining several lessons. Skipping key fundamentals makes learning improbable, if not impossible. Skipping steps also has an effect opposite to the one you want, because learning is slowed down rather than speeded up.

Daily Planning

Use the **Practice Planning Guide** to plan your daily practice. It allows for great variation. There is a definite rationale for the **lesson order**; it is not random. Choose lessons from the **lesson section** as you would courses from a Chinese restaurant menu to teach the appropriate **lesson skill** topic. Keep in mind that I wrote the lessons in descending order of importance for the most part; sections 1 to 3 are more fundamental than sections 5 to 7. Within each skill section, the lessons also increase in difficulty. The **Time Needed** is a range that you must coordinate with the time ranges (for introduction and daily practice) given in the **Coach's Corner** section of each lesson. Young or inexperienced players need more time to complete any lesson; experienced players need less time. The introductory times for any lesson are nearly double the daily practice times. So initially, since all lessons are introductory, you will have a difficult time precisely following the guide.

THE PRACTICE PLANNING GUIDE

Order Number

1. Individual Warm-Ups

The time spent on *individual warm ups* is extremely valuable. Ideally, players work on the skills they need most. Give individual instruction. Devise individual practice plans. If players work hard, extend the warm up; it will reduce the time needed for other lessons. Hopefully, players will continue to practice the same way on their own.

Practice Planning Guide

Order Number	Lesson Skill	Lesson Section	Time Needed (minutes)
1	individual warm-ups	any 1-13	5-15
2	continuous movement (continuous motion)	1.2+,1.3, 9.32, 9.4+	15-30
3	individual skills - new lessons	1-13	15-30
4	shooting technique	3, 5-8	10-30
5	defense	12, 11.3	10-15
6	individual skills, transition, team	1-13, 14-19	10-15
7	lay ups	5.4-5.5, 5.8	5-10
8	warm down	see Appendix B	5-10
9	individual practice	any 1-13	0-20
TOTALS			75-175
APPROXIMATE AVERAGE			~2 HOURS

During warm-ups watch and work with players; this is not time for a coffee break. Watch for players shooting from great distances, practicing incorrectly, or wasting time. Given individual instruction, players readily recognize the great value of this time.

2. Continuous Movement

The *continuous motion lesson* conditions your players cardiovascularly while they practice many basic skills. You will need several days of introductory lessons, before running a continuous motion lesson. Initially, players perform simple ball handling skills while constantly moving for 15 minutes. Players need just move, not sprint. Gradually extend the length to 30 minutes. The complexity of the skills practiced can also increase.

Practice the continuous motion lesson first, because it is a good warm up. Do it before any sprinting. It also enables players to focus better at practice, just as jogging does for adults. After this warm up, players are ready to slow down and listen for a while. This is an opportune time, while the players are fresh, to teach something new.

3. Individual Skill, New Lesson

Initially, all lessons are new. So, several weeks might elapse before you introduce only one new lesson each day. Meanwhile use this time to teach individual skills not included in other parts of practice. These include pivoting, dribbling, and the going-for-the-ball skills–catching, passing, and cutting.

Pivoting and dribbling have priority over the going-for-the-ball skills. Pivoting is the last part of any going-for-the-ball skill, so players need pivoting expertise to complete any of these. Dribbling is a skill that players enjoy practicing on their own. So, teach dribbling as soon as possible. It is also part of many other lessons, especially the shooting lessons. After the first several weeks the team may need to spend little time on separate dribbling lessons.

4. Shooting Technique

After a difficult new lesson do an easy one. Shooting technique is easy to practice, not easy to perform well. Teaching it requires close supervision. Shooting technique, like dribbling, is happily practiced by players in warm-ups and outside practice. So, it is advantageous to teach it as soon as possible.

5. Defense

Defensive lessons require a maximum physical effort. This is a physically difficult lesson after an easy one. Players use little skill and thought so these lessons are easy to learn. Hustle (heart) is an integral part of all defensive lessons.

6. Individual Skill or Transition or Team

For the first several days, or weeks, teach individual skills in this slot. When players are ready, start teaching the team skills. You can also introduce team skills, especially transition lessons, in the new lesson slot as well.

7. Layups

Do layups as a team to end practice. Encourage the players to loudly count each shot made in a row. After making the required number from the left, right, and center positions, end the practice. This tactic wraps up practice on an up note.

8. Warm Down

Before players leave we have a warm down which involves stretching, cooling off, and talking. (See warm down in appendix.)

9. Individual Practice

Any individual practice after this needs to focus on a lesson, no playing or just shooting around since players do this enough on their own.

The Total Practice

Plan to spend 2 hours for a practice planned like the guide. The minimums and maximums for each section when added up indicate that practice can vary from about 1 hour (75 minutes) to 3 hours (175 minutes). Adjust the time spent on each lesson based on the needs of your players. A stop watch is helpful. If you spend additional time on the current lesson then partially cut one or several of the following lessons. With young players at the beginning of the season things will probably vary greatly. It takes a while before you can follow a complete practice plan. It is okay if you only complete half of the practice. Your kids need the time on the basics. You need time to learn what your players need.

There are several things you can do to help cut practice time:

- Encourage players to practice the lessons on their own.
- Give practice lessons as homework. For example, tell a player to do 100 pivots or take 50 one-foot shots.
- Use the warm-ups to full advantage to

reduce the time needed for regular practice lessons.

- Cut the time for a lesson done frequently.
- Introduce less new material. Never rush if you are behind schedule.
- It is okay to go into preseason games without teaching the center jump or press, etc.
- Plan to teach on game day while waiting for referees or the other team. Often there is 30 minutes of usable time.
- Plan teaching sessions before and even during a preseason scrimmage.

The schedule is always tight if you teach the fundamentals. Planning again is the key. The results are obvious.

Seasonal Planning

Looking at the great number of skills and lessons (over 170) can be overwhelming unless you do some seasonal planning. In particular, you need to plan weeks or even months ahead to teach each team skill. You don't have to stick to this schedule. Your plans will surely change, but this gives you reachable goals and a sensible framework to teach the individual skills. Planning the individual skills is easier; just go in order from the easiest one to the most difficult one. Alternate days and the amount of time spent on each lesson, so at the end of the week or month players have a complete dose.

The first team skill taught is a defensive center jump setup. Players learn this lesson in 15 minutes and do not require repeated practice. Because it is not a critical lesson, you can practice it any time before the first game. Teach the foul line setup next. Use this setup to teach boxing out and the transition game as well. Get to this as soon as possible.

Young players have very different needs than older high school players. The foul line transition and helping out on defense lessons are the only critical team skills for younger players. Be patient and wait to teach plays until players can cut and communicate well. The only additional critical skill for older players is offense against the press, because you will certainly be pressed if you have a lead near the end of a game.

Planning Scrimmages

Scrimmages, like games, act as tests for the players (and coach). Players want to be prepared for a test; they practice harder and listen more closely. Plan a scrimmage for the first week of practice and then immediately announce this to your players.

Schedule teams of similar ability. Great wins or losses may affect the learning process in a negative way. Eventually players understand that you care more about how they play than winning or losing. It may be a good idea not to keep a running score. Decide with the other coach how to run the scrimmage. Do you want to hire referees or referee yourself? Do you want a game or a scrimmage with 10-15 minute teaching time-outs? Do you plan to predominately use the best players or do all players play equal times? I favor self-refereed games with 10-15 minute teaching time outs for younger players initially. Self-refereeing also gives you the opportunity to spend a few extra seconds explaining calls to players and even showing them a better way to accomplish something. Game referees' seldom have time to give explanations, and they certainly will not instruct. Buy and read the rule book for your league, so you understand better the calls and rules.

Chapter Two

2

Principles of Practice Teaching

The principles of practice teaching have much to do with attitude. These methods of dealing with players derive from my deep seated beliefs, as I previously have explained.

1. Focus on individual skills. Team skills are just applications and combinations of these.

2. Write down your practice plan in a book for future reference as well as on a 3x5 card for practice. (Copy pages from the appendix.)

3. Use a stopwatch to time lessons. Don't force lessons into the allotted time. If you need more time for one lesson, cut from another. An assistant can help you time.

4. Involve all players every minute in practice. There is no sideline where unoccupied players go. Nobody sits.

5. Each player needs a ball. Any type of ball will do. Bob Cousy's signature can be missing. It can be lopsided. Use volleyballs or beach balls, if necessary. It is easy to acquire used balls from any school. They usually have closets full of old, used, lopsided balls taking up storage space, gathering dust. No excuses.

6. Do not let players dribble when lessons do not involve dribbling. Do not allow dribbling between lessons either. This activity not only wastes time, but also allows players to continue poor dribbling and looking habits. You need to supervise and control dribbling in warm-ups, practice, and warm downs especially with novice players.

7. Use what I call **shadows** when teaching team skills or skills involving many players. Shadows follow the same directions as the player you teach, only from a few feet behind. You may need to use two or more shadows sometimes. Often the shadows alternate position with the first player in line. This keeps all players actively involved and learning. The lessons instruct you when to use shadows.

8. Use all players in practice scrimmages, even if this means having 16 players on the court. The smallness of younger players readily allows this. With older, larger players you may want to limit the player number to 12 or 14.

9. Each player needs to learn the individual skills for each position. Tall players practice dribbling just like short ones. Short players learn boxing out.

10. Plant ideas in players ahead of time. It directs thinking and effort. The ideas can involve strategies in tomorrow's game, or skills that you will practice next week. Inform players when you will teach particular skills.

11. Give lessons for homework. There are many things players can practice without a court or even without a ball. (See the COURT and BALL sections of The Table of Lessons in the appendix.) If there is a ball and a court available at home, so much the better.

12. Make sure players practice correctly when you are watching. Hopefully players will continue to practice correctly on their own. Players should find practicing the way taught easy. However, there are millions of ways to do things incorrectly. Watch for these. Practicing perfectly makes perfect; practicing incorrectly facilitates bad habits that are difficult to change.

13. Do not play favorites. Good players are not better people or more important people. Bad players are not bad people. They are unique, worthwhile individuals. Treat all players as great people.

14. Keeping track of layups or short shots missed encourages players to do better. If needed, tell players how many shots they missed privately. The last resort is to make an announcement to the team. Never use this information to berate players. You can require a player to shoot 2 or 3 full court layups or shots after practice for each one missed. Keep these statistics in a book, so that you can readily peruse an entire week or month.

15. Make simple practice rules for the players.

16. Run each lesson at the appropriate effort level.

17. Be aware of the many Do Nots for coaches. See the Field Tested Mistakes section in this chapter.

18. Use managers. They are more than tremendous help; they are a necessity. Train them just like players.

19. Comment readily to a player when you see improvement. This will occur often when you use these methods.

Rules for the Players

1. Be at practice on time, dressed, ready to play.

2. Do not dribble or even hold a basketball while I (the coach) am talking or teaching a lesson. (Use *balls down* as the instruction before teaching to remind players to place all balls on the floor. Otherwise, balls slip out of players' hands causing distractions.)

3. Players may not leave the gym or a lesson without permission.

4. No 30 foot shots, or shots outside the foul line, at any time in the gym. The younger the players the closer the distance they need to practice.

5. Inform the coach of illness immediately by phone or by note.

Effort Levels of Lessons

For a lesson to be effective, you must be clear as to what physical effort is required by players. Should players shoot as if it were the game on-the-line, or should they take time squaring up and moving their arms into position? Should the defense play at 100% effort or should they offer token resistance? Each lesson in this book is run at one of the three effort levels below.

Level 1, The Technique Level–This level exaggerates the proper way to shoot, pass, dribble, etc. Perform technique level lessons slowly. Perform them this way in practice only, not in games. Practicing at this level reaps tremendous benefits. Improvement occurs in the ball skills without even using a ball. Minute for minute of practice, this is the best spent time for players. Coach for coach, these lessons are the least recognized and practiced.

Level 2, The Practice Level - Lessons at this level are the most common. Players normally practice most skills this way.

Level 3, Game Level - Game level lessons are the most advanced level of lessons. Exert game type pressure on the player. Transition and other hustle lessons that demand a maximum physical effort are game level lessons. Any offensive lesson with aggressive defense as well as all full speed defensive lessons are also game level lessons.

Using Assistants and Managers

Assistants are more than a tremendous help; they are a necessity.

•At games they set up the gym and keep score and time, as well as statistics.

•At practice they assist in a great variety of ways:

1. They act as offensive or defensive players (usually dummy) in lessons.

2. The assistant can spot such individual actions as walking violations. Assign one individually to assist a player.

3. They keep practice statistics such as number of missed layups.

4. **They** keep time using a stop watch for each lesson. Often I ask one manager to time the lessons. If one lesson takes longer than the scheduled time I need to cut back on another. The manager can inform you to stop when 5 or 10 minutes have elapsed. This keeps you approximately on schedule. Note that some lessons can readily be cut, others can't. This is one reason to use time ranges when you plan practice, instead of specific times.

5.They can keep players far apart minimizing chances of collisions and also direct traffic in lessons where players are close.

Each lesson gives other specific uses for managers.

Treat managers like players in every respect. They listen to the lessons; they do not practice shooting or dribbling on the side. They are there, ready to go, each day when you need them. They get letters, jackets, trophies, etc., just like any player. My warmest feelings toward any students are to my many basketball managers. Thanks again.

If you are a teacher, recruit your best students as managers. Older students are better managers. Use 5 or 6 managers if you can get them. Use males or females, regardless of the gender of your team. The critical selection criterion is interest. Teach one manager how to keep score or time or statistics. Then, have this manager train others. Always check on this training. As with the players, teach each manager every job. Have many keep official score at a game or scrimmage. As with players, keep them all working. Nobody just sits.

Methods That Do Not Work–Do Nots

This list could be longer than any other list in the book. There are many ways to do things poorly and ineffectively (I have tried them), fewer ways to do things well. Here are some Do Nots.

1. DO NOT play games in practice. The next section details why this is a big mistake.

2. DO NOT allow players to practice incorrectly. Make sure that they both practice needed skills and adhere to the lessons.

3. DO NOT spend much time teaching zone defenses until person-to-person is learned.

4. DO NOT practice foul shooting by taking 10 or 20 in a row. See the foul shooting technique lessons (5.6,5.7)

5. DO NOT practice shooting from more than four feet with novices, one foot is better. Use the specifically designed practice shooting lessons if you want players to practice at greater distances.

6. DO NOT have your players run without using basketball skills as they are running. No kamikaze drills (unless players dribble).

7. DO NOT get players overly excited or UP for a game. Usually they are UP. You need to do the reverse–calm players down.

8. DO NOT act nervous in games. This makes players nervous.

9. DO NOT come to practice unprepared. PLAN

10. DO NOT force players with small hands to shoot with one hand. This two-handed method is much more difficult than shooting one-handed. Players readily shoot with one hand when they are able. However, make sure they practice shooting technique with one hand. Practicing technique one handed will improve the two handed shot as well as ready players for a one handed shot.

11. DO NOT overuse praise. Players want your attention, consideration, and help. Praise is often used in lieu of these more important things.

12. Most importantly, *never think that the game is more important than any **one** of your players.*

These are just some of the Do Nots I have learned from personal experience. I'd like to hear some of yours.

Playing Games in Practice

More needs to be said about playing games in practice. It is a poor way for novices to learn or practice newly introduced individual skills. The reasons are many:

1. There is little repetition of any particular skill in a game compared to a particular lesson. Learning follows (correct) repetition. Each player may only take 5 shots in a 30 minute game, whereas each player can take 30 shots in two minutes of shooting practice. The same holds for the other skills as well.

2. Repetition in a game is not timely. Shooting for example, does not take place at regular short spaced intervals. Learning needs uninterrupted repetitions.

3. At any instant in a game, a coach will find it difficult to coach 10 players simultaneously, because each one moves uniquely. It is easy to allow players to continue to make errors.

4. In a game players use skills combined in groups. Players learn best when you teach each skill separately and then further break each skill into its components. Combine the skills after each is learned, not before.

Playing Street Ball-Half Court Basketball Outside of Practice

When I grew up playing half court, two-on-two and three-on-three, was very common, much more common than full court games. The basketball experience obtained by playing half court is useful, especially for developing individual moves, but not nearly as helpful as proper practice. Consider the number of playground players and the amount of time they spend on the court. If street ball were that worthwhile there would be many more stars coming off the playgrounds right into the college and pro ranks. This rarely, if ever, occurs. The fact that foreign players often play with great skill, despite their lack of street ball experience compared with Americans, only confirms this belief. Here are some reasons why playing too much street ball is a Do Not for players:

1. Conditioning usually does not take place because of the lack of continuous movement.

2. An important part of the game, the transition game, is not part of half court play.

3. Team play is not encouraged, since a player is always close enough to the basket to score.

4. Playing more rested in a half court game and then playing after sprinting down the court a few times are quite different.

5. Injuries are much more likely to happen in half court games, because there are so many quick direction changes.

6. Three second rules usually never apply in these games. So half court offenses do not work in real games.

There is no need to tell your players that half court is no good. Instead, encourage them to play full court outside practice, even if it is only two-on-two or one-on-one. Encourage players as well to use the three second rule in any type of game; tell them that other players may abide by this rule if someone calls this obvious violation. Most importantly, encourage players to practice the way you teach them.

Chapter Three

3

Strategies with Players Plus

A. Walking into a New Gym

One disadvantage of playing away games is that the gym and surroundings are different. At Overbrook High School in 1963, the gym was more than minuscule. I still remember the stunned look on the face of a tall opponent *snuffed* by gymnastic rings hanging down from the ceiling. Swollen palms and elbows resulted from banging off small portions of wall that intruded onto the court near the baskets.

At more modern gyms, there are still problems. Often, I found holes in the floor and warped floors because of ceiling leaks. Often there were dead spots on the floor. Usually, schools use gyms for so many sports that the overlapping court lines make it difficult to tell the badminton border from the basketball endline. Court sizes vary as well. Regulation-size courts can be 50% larger than the puny one you practice on. Background lighting, as well as solid or glass backboards, affect shooting. Unexpectedly having to look into a sunny window (or bright TV lights) while shooting is another obstacle to overcome. These anomalies cause violations, lost balls, missed shots, and more, often critical situations.

There is an easy way to avoid many of these problems. Walk around the court with your team before the game, before the players even change. Walk single file on the sidelines and endlines. Point out any problem and/or difficulties detected as a group. Players feel more comfortable on the court after this stroll. They also recognize boundaries, bad spots, and many other court idiosyncrasies.

B. Game Warm-Ups

Use warm-ups for more than just loosening up the bones. In a game most players rarely handle the ball, so players need to warm up ball handling skills as well. Since warm-up time is limited, use efficient drills. The regular layup drill is not one of them, because players stand around most of the time. All players need a ball, just like practice. Practice shooting technique, one-foot shots, layups, and passing. With novices, practice pivoting and other beginning skills just as you do in practice. Use this time wisely. Here are some suggestions (use any extension as well):

Game Warmups		
#	**Skill**	**Lesson**
1.	Shooting technique	5.0, 5.1
2.	Shooting practice	5.3
3.	Layups	5.4, 5.5, 5.8
4.	Passing	9.7, 9.1

C. Substituting

Games are for players; daily practice is for the coach. Gametime is the only time for players to apply practice teachings. Play as many players as possible for at least a quarter. Mix better players with the others in the lineup. Inform players in practice that they will report in for so-and-so. This is a time of learning and development for players, not a time to let your ego run wild. Benching players because you have to win creates lifelong scars.

D. Time-outs

Take time-outs to relay information to your players. Take one just after the start of the game if players are confused. In tight situations, decide if the time-out will help the other team more than your own. A well-coached team may be better off not calling a time-out if the other team will benefit more.

Talk slowly in time-outs. Base instructions on the players' skills; players must possess the ability to successfully execute them. Often I knew exactly what my players needed to do. Unfortunately, they did not have the skills (yet) to do so. In one case, after one week of practice, players (11th and 12th graders) did not know how to cut to the ball. The opponent's press squashed us. I once taught players (10th grade) a 2-1-2 shifting zone defense during a time-out, only because these players possessed all the needed skills.

Remain overtly calm and light, especially in tight situations; players mimic you. If you are uptight, players will play this way. Calm coaching reaps great reward. My uptight record for close (one or two point) games is 0-7 (my first full season); my calm record is about 20-1.

What if you need to relay much information to your players? Inform the refs ahead of time that you will take another time-out after the first one. Assign a manager to time it, using a stop watch, to insure that anxious refs do not cut 15 seconds or so off the second one. Young players often do not understand clipboard explanations. It is okay to bring them out on the court to describe a new setup. Even if the other team pays attention, which is not very probable, they still need to figure out what you are talking about and then plan a counter strategy. I'd worry more about being hit by lightning.

E. Psychology

Pregame

Players always seem to be up for games. Never tell players how important a game is to you; it's your problem. Players must concentrate on their specific job. Plant ideas the day before the game. Direct players to focus on two things at most. Better, just one. Never discuss standings unless asked. This is the job of sportscasters. Players intuitively know if a game is important. Emphasizing the point psyches them out. For example, bet 50 cents on a shot. Take it, and then bet one million dollars on the same shot. It won't be the same. Fifty-cent shots are easier.

Game

Stay cool. All games are for the players. Success or failure has already occurred at practice. Here you can only score more or fewer points than the other team. This is hardly significant, especially since your players can play well and lose and play poorly and win. Expert planning yields predictable results; players do exactly the same in games as they do at practice. Surprises and anger suggest poor planning.

F. Dealing with Referees

Referees possess a variety of abilities. A coach can only hope for consistent calling. Sometimes consistent calls work against your team. For example, referees decide they are not going to call all the fouls because they have experienced so much fouling with players at this level. You have taught your team not to foul or hack. The result is that the other team is hacking the heck out of your team; the refs only call one of every five fouls. This gives the other team a great advantage.

What do you do? The refs are probably not aware that one team is hacking and the other isn't. Point it out to them. Tell them that your players do not flail their arms or hack. The hacking is one way and this is putting your team at an unfair disadvantage. Most refs notice this immediately and then call more fouls on the hackers.

If you do not understand a call or you think the refs have made a mistake, attempt to get an explanation. If you can't get the refs' attention on an important matter call a time-out. Before discussing the problem, state that you want an official time-out because there is a mistake. If the ref agrees after the parley, you get the official time-out. If not, you get to explain yourself and find out what the refs are thinking. Usually, they are decent people who want what is best for everybody. You can also ask a ref about a less important call at halftime or after the game.

Never argue. Understand their rationale. Inform them of yours. Usually the bad calls will balance out by the end of the game. If they don't, raise hell during the game and, especially, after it. Refs with chips on their shoulders will penalize your team more unless the other ref works to even things out.

G. Locker Room Talks

Let's set the scene. The locker room; halftime; your team is down by 10; players sit on benches with sweaty, dispirited faces. Ronald Reagan comes in and gives an inspiring talk that ends with, "Let's do it for the Gipper." Faces radiate energy, the sweating stops, veins explode from muscles raring to go; the team rejuvenates. Your team beats the crap out of the opponent in the second half. …only in the movies. Even Geritol can't help your team (or you). Winning and losing are not even the problem; quality of play is. There are no surprises in games unless you have problems every day in practice. Take care of problems in practice.

Never did I experience players who needed a pep talk. The bigger problem is keeping players calm and focused. You can only do this if you are calm and focused. Planning ahead helps.

H. Keeping Statistics

If possible, have an assistant keep game statistics. See the Appendix on statistics for more specific information. The most important statistic is the offensive rebounds by the opposing team. These lead to easy scores. The next is turnovers and violations by your team. Other important statistics are shooting and foul shooting percentage, and offensive and defensive rebounds.

Use these numbers for planning your practices, not to beat your players with. It is foolish to tell your players that they need to practice shooting, for example. You plan the practices. Shooting poorly is a result of your poor teaching and planning. So, beat yourself, not your players. Give players any statistics they want. They are not secret information.

I. The Beginning of the Season

A. Choosing a Team

Teach as many players as you can handle. The methods in this book allow you to handle twice as many players as you might have initially thought you could. Give players ample opportunity to cut themselves before you do it. Wait 2-4 weeks before cutting a team down to a minimum level. Twelve may be a nice number, an even dozen, for a team, but if you carry 15 players you can field three complete teams. This is easier than figuring out what to do with those two extras. The only thing special about the number 12 is that they sell donuts cheaper by the dozen.

If 12 is such an optimal number for teaching, why do school districts assign 30-60 students to normal classes?

B. Choosing Assistants

Assistants are of great help. Given specific directions, just as you give to players, assistants enhance your efforts. A talented assistant may be able to handle players as well as you. Five or six assistants are not too many. If necessary, use them as a dummy team. Choose assistants as you do players. High schoolers can be a great help with players at any level. Usually they have an interest in basketball, so they listen closely and often work with the team. Adults, on the other hand, can be a problem. Most sports aficionados and even coaches think they know it all without any study or preparation. Make it clear that you are going to follow these methods (this book plus whatever) and that you want them to do so as well. If they think *winning is the only thing* direct them to the closest professional team that needs assistants.

Chapter 4–Warm Down

Tight muscles not only slow down a player, but also increase the chance for injury. Since muscles tighten after a work out, a warm down afterwards to loosen muscles is essential.

This warm down with a few strengthening exercises is similar to the one I used. As soon as possible, assign one player to lead it. The coach watches and talks during a long stretch. Emphasize that players should perform the exercises gently, using steady pressure– jerky or forced movements can cause injury. The goal is to gradually extend the range of muscle movement. Players inhale during the first part of an exercise, like a sit up, and exhale when lowering to the original position. Make sure players know the goal for the exercise. Joe Fareira, a veteran track coach from the Philadelphia area, assisted me in developing this warm down.

Two sets of muscle groups are mentioned often in the exercises. The **hamstrings** are located at the back of the thigh. The **quadriceps** are located at the front outside of each thigh.

# NAME	DIRECTIONS	DIAGRAM
1 Hurdler's Stretch	Start this common runners' stretch sitting on the floor with both feet straight out in front of you, knees straight. Bend the right thigh back so that it makes an L with the other foot. This may be very difficult, so instruct players to go only as far as possible. Bend the calf towards the body. See the Diagram. Bend forward at the waist as far as possible. Hold the ankle or the furthest part on the leg that can be reached for 10 seconds. This stretches the hamstrings. Lay backward as far as possible from this same position for 10 seconds to stretch the quadriceps. Repeat this with the right leg forward.	
2 Feet over head	Lie down with the back on the floor. Bring the legs straight up together and back over the head. Try to touch the floor with your toes. Hold this position for 10 seconds. See diagram. Lower the legs slowly to the floor. This exercise strengthens the lower back.	
3 Sit-ups	Do 10 sit-ups slowly with the legs bent. Inhale as you count to 4 on the roll up and exhale counting to 4 as you roll down. Have a partner hold the feet down if there is nothing to put their feet under. This strengthens the mid-section and lower back.	hold feet

Warm Down continued

# / NAME	DIRECTIONS	DIAGRAM
4 Back ups	Lie on the stomach, arms behind the back. Bring the chest and head upwards. Inhale, counting to 4 on the way up, and then exhale, counting again to 4 on the way down. Do 5 slowly. This strengthens the stomach area.	initial motion
5 Back stretch	Lie on stomach. Bend calves up and extend arms behind back to grab feet. Pull for 10 seconds. Repeat. This stretches back, arms and other parts of body.	back stomach
6 Twister	Standing up with hands behind head, slowly rotate downward to the left. At the halfway point the head is between the legs as close to the ground as possible. Continue rotating upward to the right to the original position. Keep the legs in one position while rotating; if your legs are straight, keep them straight, if bent, keep them bent. Count to 6 or 8 on each rotation. Repeat, rotating in the opposite direction. Do 3 times.	rotate from the waist
7 Toe touches(3)	(1) With the feet together, bend from the waist and touch your toes. Hold for 10 seconds. (2) Repeat this with the feet far apart. This time hold the left foot with both hands for 10 seconds. Repeat, holding the right foot. (3) For a third stretch, crisscross the feet first one way, then the other. The back foot is stretched in this exercise. These stretch all muscles up to the hip.	together straddled crossed
8 Push up	Start on the knees and walk with the hands to a push up position. Do a push up and walk back. Repeat 3 times.	
9 Windmills	From a standing position rotate both arms forward (Clockwise) making a circle with the hands. Repeat 10 times. Rotate the arms 10 times in the opposite direction.	

Warm Down continued

# NAME	DIRECTIONS	DIAGRAM
10 Head rotations	Rotate the head from left to down to right to back. Count to 6 on each rotation. Repeat 3 times. This exercise relieves tension.	top view
11 Hamstring exercise	Place the heel of one foot forward on a raised object 3 feet off the ground. Lean forward, keeping the leg straight. Grab ankle and hold for 5-10 seconds. Repeat, raising the other foot. Use a partner to hold the foot if no objects are around. Repeat again.	
12 Quadriceps exercise	Stand near a wall or object you can touch for balance. Raise one foot behind and grab it with the same side arm. Lift gently. Hold for 5-10 seconds and then repeat, using the other foot and arm. Repeat again.	
13 Wall leans (3)	(1) With feet one yard from the wall, lean towards the wall keeping the heels on the floor and the legs straight. Hold for 5-10 seconds. This stretches the Achilles tendon and the calf. (2) Repeat this with your toes on a 3 inch high piece of wood or other object. You want the heels to be lower than the toes. Hold for 10 seconds. (3) Now step forward with one foot and raise the other off the ground. Hold for 10 seconds and repeat with the other foot. This also stretches the Achilles tendon and the calf.	(1) (2) (3)

Chapter 5—Statistics

This is a simple way for a coach or manager to keep a detailed record of what occurred in a game. You can also use these statistics in case the official scorers make a mistake with fouls, points, or time-outs. Usually I also assign a manager to keep unofficial score on a copy of the official score sheet as an additional precaution.

Many helpful statistics can be calculated using this information. Here is an explanation of how to use the form and analyze the statistics. Blank sheets for your use follow.

Use the following abbreviations to detail game action. Put the letter in the Us or Opponent box in the chart. Continue in order, left to right, top to bottom as you fill out the chart. When a quarter or half ends draw a dark line and use the next open line to write the new letter.

J—won jump   R—rebound. Offensive if after a shot.

X—missed shot, X^F—fouled on shot   2—made shot

0—missed foul shot   1—made foul shot

T—turnover, bad pass, lost ball   V—violation, 3 seconds, walking

F—non-shooting foul

?—missed or do not understand what happened. Write what happened if there is time.

Sample Data with Interpretation

Line	Opponent	Us
1	J X R 2	2
2	X	R 2
3	X R V	T
4	X^F 0 1	X R X R X R 2
5		

Interpretation

LINE 1 The opponent won the jump(J), missed a shot(X), got the offensive rebound(R), then made the shot(2). In our next possession we took a shot and made it(2). If we had gotten possession after the jump, then the opponent's box on **line 1** would be empty.

LINE 2 In their next possession, the opponent missed the shot(X). We got the rebound(R). This is a defensive rebound. At the other end of the court, we made the shot(2).

LINE 3 On their next possession our opponents missed a shot(X), got another offensive rebound(R), then walked or committed a violation(V). We then turned the ball over(T) as our team came down the court.

LINE 4 We fouled an opponent on a missed shot(X^F). Do not count missed shots as shots when a player is fouled. The first foul shot was missed(0). The second one was made(1). On our possession we shot three times(X's), pulled down 3 offensive rebounds(R's), and then scored(2).

Analysis

At the end of the game or quarter, you can analyze this information. The darker an area is shaded the more important this statistic category. All rebounding is important. Because the opponent's offensive rebounds usually lead to easy scores I consider this the most important statistic. Our turnovers, violations, shooting percentages, and fouls committed are other important numbers. Note that the analysis of these statistics will help you more in planning practice than in a game.

SUMMARY OF GAME STATISTICS		
Type	**Opponent**	**Us**
OFFENSIVE REBOUNDS	2	3
DEFENSIVE REBOUNDS	1	1
TURNOVERS	0	1
VIOLATIONS	1	0
JUMPS WON	1	0
SHOTS MADE	1	3
SHOTS MISSED	3	3
SHOOTING %	1/4, 25%	3/6, 50%
FOULS MADE	1	0
FOULS MISSED	1	0
FOUL SHOT %	1/2, 50%	0
FOULS BY	0	1

Game Statistics

Use the below abbreviations to detail the game action.

J - won jump	R - rebound.	X - missed shot
2 - made shot	0 - missed foul shot	1- made foul shot
F - non-shooting foul	T - turnover, lost ball	V - violation, 3 seconds, walking

? - missed or do not understand. Write what happened if there is time.
Circle multiple foul shots. Write the quarter or half number on the next open line.

Date_____ Us_____ Opponents_____ Played at_____

Line	Us	Them	Us	Them
1				
2				
3				
4				
5				
6				
7				
8				
9				
10				
11				
12				
13				
14				
15				
16				
17				
18				
19				
20				
21				
22				
23				
24				
25				
26				
27				
28				
29				
30				
31				
32				
33				
34				
35				
36				

Summary of Game Statistics User Form

At the end of the game or quarter you can analyze this information. The shaded areas indicate what I think most important. Compare the shooting and foul information with the official score sheet.

SUMMARY OF GAME STATISTICS		
Type	**Opponent**	**Us**
OFFENSIVE REBOUNDS		
DEFENSIVE REBOUNDS		
TURNOVERS		
VIOLATIONS		
JUMPS WON		
SHOTS MADE		
SHOTS MISSED		
SHOOTING %		
FOULS MADE		
FOULS MISSED		
FOUL SHOT %		
FOULS BY		

Inside Shot Statistics

The ideal percentage of shots taken inside varies from game to game, team to team, and from young to old. Work for over 50%; 100% is great; 0% stinks. In any case you want to shoot more inside shots than your opponents.

How to Use the Statistic

Instruct a manager to put a small x for a missed shot or a small two (2) for a shot made on the diagram at the corresponding spot on the court where the shot was taken. Don't worry about being slightly off. It is more important to record every shot. Switch to the next diagram when the current one is full, or at the next half or quarter. Make sure to show your manager the **inside area** on the actual court.

How to Calculate the Statistic

Count the total number of shots both made and missed in each quarter, half, or game. Calculate the percentage of inside shots made using this formula:

$$\frac{\text{inside shots}}{\text{total shots}} \times 100$$

What the Statistic Means

There are no absolutes with this statistic because of the many variables such as the age and ability of the players. So, use it on a relative scale to compare your team to the opponent, though the inside percentage of your team should be over 50%.

If your inside percentage is low or lower than the other team, it could mean several things:

1. Your team is not looking to work the ball inside.

2. Your players have not mastered the basic offensive skills in section 9 (Passing) and 10 (Catch-cut technique).

3. Your team is not rebounding well, especially offensively.

If the opponent's inside percentage is high or higher than yours, then it could mean that your team is not playing defense well. Work on overplaying, boxing out, and helping out.

INSIDE SHOT STATISTICS

Use a small X for a missed shot or a small two (2) for a shot made. Be accurate.
You do not need to be exact. Record all shots.

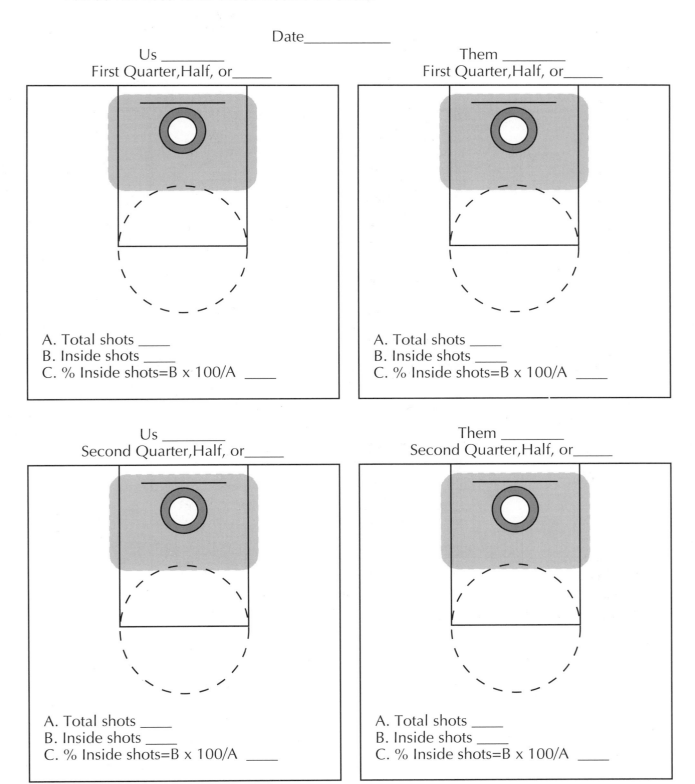

Date_____

Us _____
First Quarter,Half, or_____

Them _____
First Quarter,Half, or_____

A. Total shots _____
B. Inside shots _____
C. % Inside shots=B x 100/A _____

A. Total shots _____
B. Inside shots _____
C. % Inside shots=B x 100/A _____

Us _____
Second Quarter,Half, or_____

Them _____
Second Quarter,Half, or_____

A. Total shots _____
B. Inside shots _____
C. % Inside shots=B x 100/A _____

A. Total shots _____
B. Inside shots _____
C. % Inside shots=B x 100/A _____

Sample Practices

Order Number	Reccomended Lesson	First Day 6-8 grade	First Day 9-11 grade	First Day 12+ grade	1-2 months later 9-11	Mid season 9-11
1	individual warm-ups any 1-13 5-15 minutes	watch 5 minutes		work with players 10-30 minutes		
2	continuous movement 1.2+,1.3, 9.32, 9.4+ 15-30 minutes	skip		1.2+ext	1.2+ext 1.3	9.3,9.4
3	individual skills new lessons,1-13 15-30 minutes	1.0,2.0	1.0,2.0 2.1	1.0, 2.0+ext	15.2	19.0
4	shooting technique 3,5-8 10-30 minutes	3.0,5.0 5.1	3.0,5.0 5.1+ext	3.0,5.0 5.1+,5.3	5.1+,5.32 5.6	5.0-5.3, 5.6,5.7
5	defense 12, 11.3 10-15 minutes	12.0	12.0, 12.1	12.0, 12.1	12.2-3 12.6	12.21, 12.5-6
6	individual skills, 1-13 transition, team 14-19 10-15 minutes	9.0,9.1	9.0,9.1	9.0,9.1 9.11-12	9.6,10.6 15.2	10.8, 15.2
7	layups 5.4-5.5,5.8 5-10 minutes	5.41-2	5.41-2	5.41,5.44 5.5,5.51	5.51,5.8	5.51,5.8
8	warm down see Appendix B 5-10 minutes	can skip	do	do	do	do
9	individual practice any 1-13 0-20 minutes	work with players individually				

Adjust lesson times during the practice based on player need. Use a stopwatch. The maximum recommended practice is 2 hours.

User Forms

Practice Planning Guide

Order Number	Reccomended Lesson	Lesson	Time Needed (minutes)
1	individual warm-ups any 1-13 5-15 minutes		
2	continuous movement 1.2+,1.3, 9.32, 9.4+ 15-30 minutes		
3	individual skills new lessons,1-13 15-30 minutes		
4	shooting technique 3,5-8 10-30 minutes		
5	defense 12, 11.3 10-15 minutes		
6	individual skills, 1-13 transition, team 14-19 10-15 minutes		
7	layups 5.4-5.5,5.8 5-10 minutes		
8	warm down see Appendix B 5-10 minutes		
9	individual practice any 1-13 0-20 minutes		
TOTALS- 2 Hour Maximum			

User Forms

Order Number	Reccomended Lesson	MON	TUES	WED	THUR	FRI
	# Weekly Practice Planner					
1	individual warm-ups any 1-13 5-15 minutes					
2	continuous movement 1.2+,1.3, 9.32, 9.4+ 15-30 minutes					
3	individual skills new lessons,1-13 15-30 minutes					
4	shooting technique 3,5-8 10-30 minutes					
5	defense 12, 11.3 10-15 minutes					
6	individual skills, 1-13 transition, team 14-19 10-15 minutes					
7	layups 5.4-5.5,5.8 5-10 minutes					
8	warm down see Appendix B 5-10 minutes					
9	individual practice any 1-13 0-20 minutes					
	TOTALS- 2 Hour Maximum					

If the total is more than 2 hours, then adjust the time for each lesson based on player need during practice. Use a stopwatch.

Chapter Seven

7

Coach's Table of Lessons

Table Explanation

All of the table features are discussed in more detail in other sections and are also part of each lesson.

Lesson # and Name
The lessons are listed in order with the first lesson in each section in bold. The name of the first lesson in each section denotes the type of skill involved.

Players
The players needed in each group involved in the lesson. Note that the directions are given for many groups.

Court and Ball
X means you need a court or a ball for this lesson. A dash (-) means you do not.

Effort Level
1=little physical activity, technique level lesson

2=moderate activity, practice level

3=maximum physical effort involved, game level

Lessons Before
These lessons are needed before you do the current one. Usually only the lesson before is needed. However, sometimes many other lessons are needed, and it would be difficult to complete the current lesson without them.

Intro Time and Daily Time
The Intro Time is the time needed to teach a lesson for the first time. Usually it is double the Daily Time, the time needed after players understand the lesson.

Coach's Table of Lessons

LESSON #	NAME	PLAYERS	COURT	BALL	EFFORT	LESSONS BEFORE	LESSON #	INTRO TIME	DAILY TIME
1.0	**Holding the Ball**	1	-	x	1	none	**1.0**	5-10	1-2
1.1	Take Away	2	-	x	1	1.0	1.1	5-10	1-5
1.11	Hold High	2	-	x	1	1.1	1.11	-	1-5
1.12	Hold Low	2	-	x	1	1.1	1.12	-	1-5
1.2	Grab Full Court	2	x	x	2	1.1, 5.4	1.2	10-20	10-20
1.21	Short Pass Full Court	2	x	x	2	1.2	1.21	-	10-20
1.22	Tricky Pass Full Court	2	x	x	2	1.2	1.22	-	10-20
1.3	Line Lesson	T	x	x	2-3	1.1, 1.2	1.3	15-55	5-15
1.4	Move Ball	2	-	x	3	1.1	1.4	5-10	2-5
2.0	**Start Pivoting**	1	-	-	1	none	**2.0**	10-15	5-10
2.1	Pivoting with Ball	1	-	x	2	1.0, 2.0	2.1	15-20	2-20
2.2	Pivot with Defense	2	-	x	3	1.4, 2.1, 7.1	2.2	15-20	5-10
2.21	Pivot with D Pass	2+	x	x	3	2.2	2.21	10	5-10
2.22	Pivot 2 on D	3	x	x	3	2.21	2.22	10	5-10
2.23	Pivot 2 on D Pass	3+	x	x	3	2.22	2.23	10	5-10
3.0	**Flick of the Wrist - Shoot,Pass,Dribble**	1	-	-	1	none	**3.0**	10-15	2
4.0	**Dribbling D Position**	1	-	x	1	3.0	**4.0**	5-10	1-2
4.1	Look at the Leader 1-2	1+	x	x	2	4.0	4.1	20-30	5-15
4.11	Look and Count	1+	-	x	2	4.1	4.11	"	"
4.12	Watch the Game	1+	-	x	2	4.1	4.12	-	-
4.13	Twist Around	1	-	x	2	4.1	4.13	-	5-15
4.2	Follow the Leader	1+	-	x	2	4.1, 4.13	4.2	15-20	5-15
4.21	Follow Step Ahead	1+	-	x	2	4.2	4.21	-	5-15
4.22	Follow Back & Sideways	1+	-	x	2	4.2	4.22	-	1-5
4.23	Twister	1	-	-	2	4.22	4.23	5-10	1-5
4.24	Twister with Ball	1	-	x	2	4.23	4.24	-	5-10
4.3	Protect Ball	2	-	x	2-3	4.2	4.3	10-25	5-10
4.31	Protect with 2 on D	3	-	x	3	4.3	4.31	-	5-10
4.32	Dribbler Vs Dribbler	2	-	x	2	4.3	4.32	-	10-20
4.4	Dribble with D Layup	1+	x	x	2-3	4.3, 5.41	4.4	15-25	10-20
4.5	Dribble Pass with D	3	-	x	3	4.4, 9.3, 9.6, 10.5	4.5	20-30	10-20
4.51	Dribbler Shoots Ball	3	x	x	3	4.5	4.51	-	10-20
4.52	With D on Cutter	4	x	x	3	4.5	4.52	-	10-20
5.0	**Shot Technique Wrists**	1	-	-	1	none	**5.0**	10-15	2
5.1	Flick Up	1	-	x	1	5.0	5.1	10-20	2-5
5.11	Opposite Hand Flick Up	1	-	x	1	5.1	5.11	-	2-5
5.12	Flick Up High	1	-	x	1	5.1	5.12	-	2-4
5.13	Shoot Up	1	-	x	2	5.12	5.13	-	1-2
5.2	One-Inch Shot	1	x	x	1	5.13	5.2	10-30	5-10
5.3	One-Foot Shot	1	x	x	2	5.2	5.3	10-20	5-15
5.31	Regular One-Foot Shot	1	x	x	2	5.3	5.31	-	5-10
5.32	One-Foot Shot +Dribble	1+	x	x	2	4.3	5.32	-	5-15
5.33	One-Foot Jump Shot	1+	x	x	2	5.31	5.33	-	5-10

Coach's Table of Lessons continued

LESSON #	NAME	PLAYERS	COURT	BALL	EFFORT	LESSONS BEFORE	LESSON #	INTRO TIME	DAILY TIME
5.4	The No-Step Layup	1	x	x	1	1.0	5.4	15-30	5-20
5.41	One-Step Layup	1	x	x	1	5.4	5.41	-	5-20
5.42	Layup Lesson	T	x	x	2	5.41	5.42	10-20	10-15
5.43	Layup with Dribble	1	x	x	2	4.2, 5.42	5.43	15-20	5-15
5.44	Layup with Passing	T	x	x	2	5.42, 9.1	5.44	15-25	5-15
5.5	One Dribble Layup	1	x	x	2	4.2, 5.42	5.5	15-25	5-15
5.51	Two Dribble Layup	1	x	x	2	5.5	5.51	-	5-15
5.6	Foul Shot Technique	1	-	x	1	5.3	5.6	10-15	2-5
5.61	Technique Short Shot	1	-	x	1	5.6	5.61	10-15	5-15
5.62	Technique Longer Shots	1	-	x	1	5.61	5.62	-	5-15
5.7	Foul Shot Practice	1	x	x	3	5.6	5.7	5-15	5-15
5.8	Lateral Layup Lesson	T	x	x	2	2.1, 5.43, 9.5, 10.61	5.8	15-25	5-15
5.81	Bounce Pass Layup	T	x	x	2	5.8	5.81	-	5-15
6.0	**Moves**	x	x	x	-	2.1, 5.3	**6.0**	5-15	0-20
6.1	Pivot Around Shoot	1	x	x	2	6.0	6.1	5-15	0-20
6.2	Pivot Backward Shoot	1	x	x	2	6.1	6.2	5-15	0-20
6.3	Step Fake Shoot	1	x	x	2	6.0	6.3	5-15	0-20
6.31	Fake Pivot Shoot	1	x	x	2	6.3	6.31	5-15	0-20
6.32	Fake Pivot Back Shoot	1	x	x	2	6.31	6.32	5-15	0-20
6.4	Pivot Fake Shoot	1	x	x	2	6.0	6.4	5-15	0-20
6.41	Pivot Fake Back Shoot	1	x	x	2	6.4	6.41	5-15	0-20
6.5	Hook Shot 1-2	1	x	x	2	6.0	6.5	5-15	0-20
6.51	Jump Hook	1	x	x	2	6.5	6.51	5-15	0-20
6.52	Hook with Fake	1	x	x	2	6.51	6.52	5-15	0-20
6.53	Step Hook	1	x	x	2	6.51	6.53	5-15	0-20
6.54	Fake Step Hook	1	x	x	2	6.52-3	6.54	5-15	0-20
6.55	Underneath Hooks	1	x	x	2	6.54	6.55	5-15	0-20
6.6	Jump Shot	1	x	x	2	6.0	6.6	5-15	0-20
6.61	Fake Jump	1	x	x	2	6.6	6.61	5-15	0-20
6.62	Fake Pivot Around Jump	1	x	x	2	6.61	6.62	5-15	0-20
6.63	Pump Fake	1	x	x	2	6.6	6.63	5-10	5-10
7.0	**Pressure Shot**	1	x	x	2-3	6.1 or 6.6	**7.0**	5-15	5-15
7.01	Pressure Shot with D	2	x	x	3	7.0	7.01	-	5-15
7.02	Pressure Shot Two	2	x	x	3	7.01, 10.3, 11.0	7.02	-	5-15
7.1	Run Stop Shoot	1	x	x	2-3	6.6	7.1	5-10	2-5
7.11	With D	2	x	x	3	7.1	7.11	-	2-5
7.12	Run Catch Shoot	2	x	x	3	7.1, 9.1 10.6	7.12	10-20	5-15
7.2	Catch Up	2	x	x	3	5.51, 7.0	7.2	5-10	5
7.3	Defense in Face Shoot	2	x	x	3	5.3	7.3	5-10	2-5
7.31	Defense in Face Rebound	2	x	x	3	7.3, 11.3	7.31	-	2-5
7.32	Fouled Shooting	1	x	x	3	7.3	7.32	-	2-5
8.0	**Practice Shooting**	-	x	x	-	-	**8.0**	-	-
8.1	Driving to the Basket	1	x	x	2	2.1, 5.51	8.1	10-15	5
8.11	Fake Then Drive	1	x	x	2	6.4, 8.1	8.11	5-10	5

Coach's Table of Lessons continued

LESSON #	NAME	PLAYERS	COURT	BALL	EFFORT	LESSONS BEFORE	LESSON #	INTRO TIME	DAILY TIME
8.12	Drive Opposite Foot	1	x	x	2	8.1	8.12	5-10	5
8.2	Full Court Shoot	1	x	x	2	4.24, 6.6, 8.1	8.2	5-10	5-15
8.3	Near to Far	1	x	x	2	5.62	8.3	-	5-15
9.0	**Passing Technique**	1	-	-	1	2.0, 3.0	**9.0**	5	1-2
9.1	Overhead Short Pass	2	-	x	1-2	9.0, 10.0	9.1	5-10	5
9.11	Side Short Pass	2	-	x	1-2	9.1	9.11	-	5
9.12	Bounce Pass	2	-	x	1-2	9.1	9.12	-	5
9.13	Pivot Away Back Pass	2	-	x	1-2	2.1, 9.1	9.13	-	5
9.2	Baseball Pass	2	x	x	2	none	9.2	5-10	5
9.3	Baseball Pass Cut	2	x	x	2	7.1, 9.2	9.3	10-15	5-10
9.31	Midcourt Cut	2	x	x	2	9.3	9.31	-	5-10
9.32	Continuous Half Court	T	x	x	2	9.31	9.32	-	5-10
9.4	Continuous Full Court	T	x	x	2	7.2, 9.3	9.4	20-30	10-20
9.41	Full Court Pass	T	x	x	2	9.4	9.41	20-30	10-30
9.5	Pivot Pass & Communication	2	-	x	2	2.1, 9.1, 10.0	9.5	10-15	5-10
9.51	Pass Communication	2	-	x	2	9.5	9.51	10-15	5
9.52	Communication 2	2	-	x	2	9.51	9.52	-	5
9.6	D Overhead Side Pass	3	-	x	2-3	2.2, 9.51, 12.0	9.6	12-25	5-10
9.61	Defense Bounce Pass	3	-	x	2-3	9.6	9.61	-	5-10
9.7	Front Weave	3	x	x	2	5.8	9.7	15-20	10
9.8	Back Weave	T	-	x	2	1.1	9.8	10-15	5
10.0	**Catch Cut Technique**	1+	-	x	1	1.0, 9.0	**10.0**	10-20	5-10
10.01	Catching Technique 2	2	-	x	1	10.0	10.01	-	5-10
10.1	"Go Fetch It"	1+	-	x	1-2	10.0	10.1	5-20	2-10
10.11	Coming to the Ball	1+	-	x	1-2	10.1	10.11	5-10	5-10
10.2	Jump to Ball	2	-	x	1-2	10.0	10.2	10-15	5-10
10.3	Loose Ball Lesson	2	-	x	3	1.1, 11.2	10.3	5-10	3-5
10.31	Go for It	2+	-	x	3	10.3	10.31	-	3-5
10.4	Catching Bad Passes	1+	-	x	2	10.2	10.4	3-8	2-5
10.5	Cut Fake Technique	1	-	-	1	none	10.5	10-20	5-15
10.51	Cutting Off A Pick	3	-	-	1	10.5	10.51	10-20	5-15
10.6	Cut to the Ball	2	-	x	2	10.2, 10.5	10.6	10-20	5-15
10.61	Cut Communication	2	x	x	2	10.6	10.61	10-20	5-15
10.7	Three Second Lesson	1	x	-	1	10.2, 10.5	10.7	3-6	3-4
10.71	Cut into Lane	2	x	x	2	10.2	10.71	10-15	5-10
10.8	Overplay the Catcher	2	x	x	3	9.5, 10.6, 12.5	10.8	10-20	5-20
10.81	Front the Catcher	3	x	x	3	9.5, 10.6, 12.4	10.81	10-20	5-20
10.82	D on Catcher, Cut	3	x	x	3	10.8	10.82	-	5-15
10.9	D Pass, Overplay Catch	4	x	x	3	9.6, 10.82	10.9	5-20	5-15
10.91	D Passer, Front Catch	4	x	x	3	9.6, 10.81	10.91	5-10	5-15
10.92	D on Catcher, Passer Cut	4	x	x	3	10.82-10.91	10.92	5-20	5-15
11.0	**Rebound Grab Ball**	2	x	-	1	1.1, 2.1	**11.0**	5-10	2-5
11.1	Watching the Ball	1	-	-	1	none	11.1	5-10	5
11.11	The Ready Position	1	-	-	1	11.1	11.11	3	1

Coach's Table of Lessons continued

LESSON #	NAME	PLAYERS	COURT	BALL	EFFORT	LESSONS BEFORE	LESSON #	INTRO TIME	DAILY TIME
11.12	Move to Rebound	1	-	-	1	11.1	11.12	5	5
11.2	Step in Front Box Out 1-2	2	x	x	3	10.3, 11.12	11.2	10-15	5-10
11.3	Blocking Boxing Out 1-2	2	x	x	3	11.2, 12.5	11.3	15-30	10-20
12.0	**Defensive Position**	1	-	-	1	4.0	**12.0**	10-20	2-4
12.1	Move in D Position	1	-	-	1	12.0	12.1	10-30	5-25
12.2	Force Left & Right1-5	2	-	-	1-2	12.1	12.2	5-10@	2-5@
12.21	Three Yard Lesson	2	-	-	2-3	12.2	12.21	15-30	5-15
12.22	Mirror Lesson	2	x	x	3	12.21	12.22	-	5-10
12.3	Trapping 1-3	3	-	-	2-3	12.21	12.3	15-25	10-15
12.31	Trapping Game	3	-	-	2-3	12.3	12.31	-	10-20
12.4	Front Keep Out of Lane	2	x	-	3	12.1	12.4	10-20	10-15
12.41	Front and Box Out	2	x	-	3	11.3, 12.4	12.41	10-15	10-15
12.5	Overplaying 1-6	2	x	-	1-3	10.7, 12.2	12.5	~5-30	~5-15
12.6	Defense the Low Post	2+	x	-	1-2	12.5	12.6	20-30	10-15
12.61	Low Post with Passing	2+	x	-	2-3	12.6	12.61	-	10-20
12.7	D on Shooter	2	x	x	2	5.3, 11.3	12.7	10-15	3-8
12.71	D on Driver	2	x	x	2-3	12.7, 12.21	12.71	10-20	5-10
12.72	2 on 1	3	x	x	3	12.7,9.52+	12.72	10-20	5-10
13.0	**Picking or Screening 1-2**	2+	x	x	1	10.6,10.51	**13.0**	10-15	5
13.01	Defensing the Pick	4	x	x	2	13.0	13.01	10-30	5-15
14.0	**Center Jump**	T	x	x	1-3	12.1,+	**14.0**	15-25	5-10
14.01	Practice Jumping	T	x	x	3	14.0,+	14.01	5-10	2-5
14.02	D at Center Jump	T	x	x	3	all 12,14.0,+	14.02	5-10	5
15.0	**Foul Line Transition1-3**	T	x	x	1-3	all-11,12,+	**15.0**	15-30@	10-20@
15.1	Center Jump Transition	T	x	x	1-3	14.0,15.0+	15.1	15-30	10-20
15.2	Play to Transition	T	x	x	2-3	9.6,15.0,16.0+	15.2	15-25	10-20
16.0	**Offense Setup 1-2**	T	x	x	1-2	all- 9,10,12,+	**16.0**	10-20@	5-10@
16.1	Plays 1,2,3	3	x	x	2	16.0,+	16.1	20-30	10-20
16.2	Figure 8	T	x	x	2	13.0,16.0-1,+	16.2	10-25	5-15
16.21	8 with Defense	T	x	x	2-3	all 12,16.2,+	16.21	-	10-15
17.0	**Defense-Helping Out 1-3**	T	x	x	1-3	all- 11,12,+	**17.0**	20-30	10-20
17.01	Help in Figure 8	T	x	x	1-3	17.0	17.01	-	10-20
17.1	2-1-2 Zone Shift	T	x	x	1-3	17.0,+	17.1	10-15	5
17.11	Half Court Trap Zone	T	x	x	1-3	17.1,+	17.11	10-20	5-10
18.0	**Out-of-Bounds Plays**	T	x	x	1-3	16.0,+	**18.0**	10-15	5-10
18.01	4 in Line	T	x	x	1-3	18.0,+	18.01	10-15	5-10
19.0	**Full Pressure Offense**	T	x	x	1-3	16,0,17.0,+	**19.0**	20-30	15-30
19.1	Trapping Zone Press	T	x	x	1-3	19.0,+	19.1	15-30	15-20
19.11	Switch Zone to 1-on-1	T	x	x	1-3	17.1,19.1,+	19.11	-	5-15

Chapter Eight

8

A Lesson from The Coach's Manual

Lesson Features (in brief)

Table

The table that begins each section is part of the larger Table of Lessons found in Appendix G. At a glance this table gives a section overview that will aid in planning. Each section table supplies the name of each lesson as well as these additional features: lessons needed before, the number of players needed, the effort level, the estimated times to both introduce and practice the lesson on a daily basis, whether you need a ball and/or a court. The Coach's Corner section of each lesson supplies much, not all, of the same information. Note that you find the introduction and daily times for the extensions only in the table, not in the lessons.

Lesson Numbering

Each section teaches one and sometimes several intertwined skills. All lessons in a section have the same starting integer number like 1.0, 1.1, and 1.2 increasing by tenths. Zero level lessons like 1.0 and 2.0 present the first and most fundamental part of each skill. Often you need only 5-10 minutes to complete it. Some lessons like 6.0, Moves, and 8.0, Practice Shooting, do not contain a drill, but explain the lessons that follow. Read this explanation before doing anything else in those sections. Extensions of a lesson are numbered by hundredths; for example, 1.11 and 1.12 are extensions of 1.1. An extension usually takes a lesson one step further. Often, it uses the identical setup for players. Sometimes extensions provide the next small step in learning. In some cases, I divide a lesson into parts, instead of using extensions, because the skills involved are closely related. In this case, the lesson name includes the number of parts like Blocking Boxing Out 1-2.

Name

A name related to each lesson serves as a descriptive mnemonic device (I almost forgot that–oops!). When skills are executed simultaneously, their names are directly coupled like Pivot Pass or One Dribble Layup, where a player dribbles (only once) in for a layup. Lessons with skills performed separately are named like Pivot With Defense or Layup With Dribble, where the dribbling is done after the layup.

Brief

In one sentence (usually) the **brief** immediately familiarizes you with the lesson by stating the action and movement involved.

Fundamental Notes

What fundamentals do you practice in the lesson? How do they relate to each other? When do you use them in a game? What is the significance of the lesson? The Fundamental Notes section discusses these questions and more.

Setup

This specifies the physical placement of the players on the court. Diagrams point out specific court locations difficult to describe.

Directions for Players

These are the step-by-step directions for your players. It is for you, but it is directed to your players. This permits the dialogue to be more readable. Instead of telling you what to tell the players I directly instruct the players. A bullet (•) precedes information directed to the coach.

Troubleshooting Teaching and Learning

What problems will you have teaching? What common problems will players have? Here are some that I have encountered. Unfortunately, you will compile a list of your own. Send them to me.

•TEACHING - These are details that you need to emphasize.

•LEARNING - These are common difficulties exhibited by players. Expect them.

Use of Assistants

These are some of the many ways to use your assistants.

Weekly Practice

Weekly practice suggests the number of times to practice a lesson each week. Practice most lessons *daily* until players are ready for the next one. (Daily does not mean every day for the entire season.) Practice others only 1-3 times each week or season or as needed.

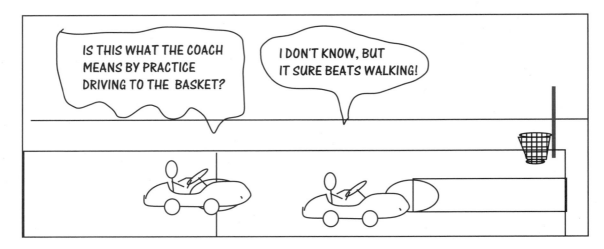

8.1 Driving to the Basket

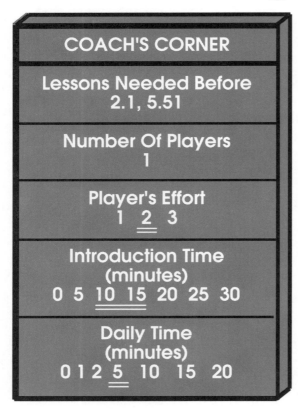

COACH'S CORNER

Lessons Needed Before
2.1, 5.51

Number Of Players
1

Player's Effort
1 <u>2</u> 3

Introduction Time
(minutes)
0 5 <u>10 15</u> 20 25 30

Daily Time
(minutes)
0 1 2 <u>5</u> 10 15 20

Brief:

From the foul line, a player drives left and right starting with either foot as the pivot.

Fundamental Notes

Players get their steps together for each drive like a hurdler getting steps together between hurdles. Righties always shoot off the left foot, and lefties off the right foot. For moments when righties use the left hand, they are considered lefties; lefties using the right hand are considered righties. Practice the four possible drives in this order (eight if you practice with both hands):

1. Left foot as pivot and go right.

2. Right foot as pivot and go right.

3. Left foot as pivot and go left.

4. Right foot as pivot and go left.

Do these at a moderate pace; no need to go fast. Encourage players to slow down if they encounter difficulty.

Setup

Each player starts at the foul line with a basketball.

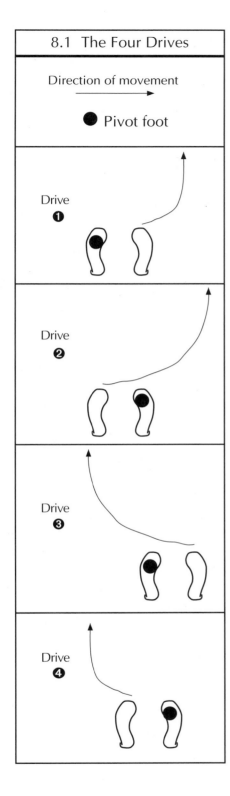

8.1 The Four Drives

Direction of movement →

● Pivot foot

Drive ❶

Drive ❷

Drive ❸

Drive ❹

Directions for Players

1. There are four possible drives.

•Name the ones you plan to introduce.

2. Start from a half down position with the ball at waist height.

•Use these directions for each drive.

3. Push the ball low, far to the side of the drive.

4. The first step is a long one, so that you can get past the defense.

5. You must step around the defense, not through them, so move sideways before moving forward. Use a chair or another person as dummy defense to step around.

•Note that drives 2 and 3 involve a crossover step.

6. Dribble the ball with the first step.

7. Do not drag the pivot foot.

8. Right handers always shoot off the left foot on either side of the basket and left handers always off the right foot.

•Novice players take as many steps and dribbles as necessary to complete the move, whereas experienced taller players can limit the steps to between 2 and 4.

9. Use only 1 or 2 dribbles. Do each drive 10 times if it feels uncomfortable, five otherwise.

•Instruct experienced players to repeat this lesson with the opposite hand.

Troubleshooting

1. Watch each player if possible.

2. Instruct a manager to stand motionless as a defensive player; a chair works just as well. The driver steps around the defense on the first step. When past, reach around and out with the inside elbow to keep the defense behind.

3. Players tend to practice quickly, so slow them down. Speed naturally increases with repetition. Players need to move at a comfortable pace while practicing.

Use of Assistants

1. Stand stationary as a defensive player to step around.

2. Watch for a dragging pivot foot.

Weekly Practice As needed

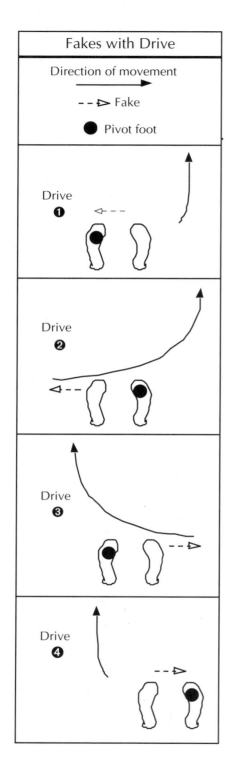

Fakes with Drive

Direction of movement →

‑ ‑ ▷ Fake

● Pivot foot

Drive ❶

Drive ❷

Drive ❸

Drive ❹

Extensions

8.11 Fake Then Drive

Players often fake before driving. The fake is executed slowly so that the defense has time to react. The defense can't react to a quick fake. Two types of fakes are used. Do each drive 5-10 times.

1. A **step fake** is used before the crossover step in drive 2 and 3 above. Slowly push the ball and the body away from the pivot foot as you step in that same direction. Bring the ball back, take the crossover step more quickly and drive to the basket. Do each drive 5 times.

2. Use a **ball body fake** for drives 1 and 4 above. Push the ball and turn the body in the opposite direction of the drive.

Then, step in the direction of the drive.

8.12 Drive Opposite Foot

This layup is taken off the wrong foot on purpose. The defense, especially tall players, are waiting for the offense to take one and a half steps before the layup. Because this opposite foot layup is shot one step sooner than expected, the defense is not ready to defend it; this is the main advantage of using it. The disadvantage is that practicing this layup undoes the fundamentals of novices and intermediate players. So, introduce this to experienced players only. Players drive to the basket like they do in lesson 8.1. This layup is usually released one step farther from the basket than normal.

Nitty-Gritty Basketball Clinics

for more or current information call 800 979 8642 or visit our website:

www.mrbasketball.net

Comments from our 1st Clinic

"The best fundamentals clinic I have attended. . . . This will give any coach more security in their knowledge of the game."

Koko Davis, Coach, Overton, NV

"I would definitely recommend this clinic to coaches- beginners or advanced!"

A. Robin Quinn, JrHS Coach, Bridgeton, NJ

"I leave with a greater knowledge and understanding of the game. More importantly, I know how to teach others the vital fundamentals that will make good players become great players."

Kasey Davis, HS Coach, Logadale, NV

"Best clinic I ever attended."

Bill Force, Morris Plains, NJ

Clinic Descriptions

Right Stuff Clinic
One Day; Oct 15, 2000 & Oct 14, 2001; for coaches all levels

Covers the most critical aspects of coaching. Dispel foolish paradigms that tell you that you just can't teach that. I will show you how to effectively teach every skill, plus how each individual skill each effects each team skill. We will also go over the most difficult to teach team skills. Both college and elementary coaches have already signed up.

Everything Clinic
Two Days; 2 days, June 23-24, 2001; coaches/players all levels

In two days I will demonstrate most individual and team skills. We will cover over 100 individual drills and most team skills. Coaches can actively participate. Players will receive individual practice routines. At our first Everything Clinic we had both college and elementary coaches and players. Min age 12.

Shooting Clinic
One day; July 7 & July 21, 2001; coaches/players, all levels

I will go over every technique needed to insure that each player improves shooting. I will also discuss many "pitfalls," so you can avoid them. I will show coaches how to overcome a variety of shooting problems and will set up a practice program for each player. We will also show you foul shooting techniques that yield dramatic improvement. **Topics covered include:** shooting technique, practice shooting, game level practice, jump shot, jump hook, opposite hand shooting, driving, moves, & foul shooting.

Defense Clinic
One day; July 8 & Aug 4, 2001; coaches/players, all levels

Defensive skills are the easiest to learn. I will show you how to effectively teach these important skills. Guaranteed improvement in just one day. Of course, more practice results in even more improvement. Bring your entire team. **Topics covered include:** Defensive position & movement, fronting, overplaying, forcing, trapping, helping out, covering shooter, & low post defense.

Offense Clinic
One day; July 22 & Aug 5, 2001; coaches/players, all levels

Everything about offense except shooting. Wondering why your plays don't work in games? I'll do more than tell you why. We will go over each individual offensive skill needed for plays to be effective as well as all other individual skills needed for offensive. Bring your team. **Topics covered include:** cutting, faking, passing, catching, plays, in bounds plays, offense vs half & full court press, and more.

Schedule for each clinic

9:30 AM —Begin Morning Session
11:30 AM —End Morning Session
12-1 —Lunch Break (1-1.5 hours) Videos
1:30 PM —Begin Afternoon Session
3:30 PM —End Afternoon Session
3:30 —Videos, Questions, Practice Programs

we've got
books, videos
and
clinics too

Nitty-Gritty Basketball Order Form

Visit our website for more current information and prices
www.MrBasketball.net

Books

A. The Basketball Coach's Bible $24.95 (07-5), 352 pgs; Everything about coaching.
B. The Basketball Player's Bible $19.95 (13-X), 270 pgs; All individual fundamentals.
C. The Basketball Shooting Guide $7.45 (30-X), 45 pgs; Yields permanent improvement.
D. The Basketball Scoring Guide $7.45 (31-8), 47 pgs; Teaches pro moves step-by-step.
E. The Basketball Dribbling Guide $7.45 (32-6), 46 pgs, Anyone can be a good dribbler
F. The Basketball Defense Guide $7.45 (33-4), 46 pgs, Defense in every situation.
G. The Basketball Pass Cut Catch Guide $7.45 (34-2), 47 pgs, Be an effective team player.
H. Basketball Fundamentals $7.45 (35-0), 46 pgs, Covers all fundamentals.
I. Planning Basketball Practice $7.45 (36-9), 46 pgs, Use time effectively, plan, plus.

Videos Available Now

All videos cost $24.95, run 40-60 minutes, and follow the books in order.

1. Fundamentals I
(77-6) Over 25 skill topics. Over 100 drills. 48 min
2. Fundamentals II
(90-3) All team skills, plays, out-of-bounds, pressure defense, plus more. 42min
3. Planning Practice I
(75-X) Goes through all practice drills. 41 min
4. Planning Practice II
(76-8) 40+ ways to get more out of practice.41 min

Videos In Production
5. Shooting I (78-4) Technique
6. Shooting II (79-2) Practice
7. Shooting III (80-6) Pressure
8. Dribbling (81-4) Everything
9. Defense I (84-9) Position, Movement, Overplay, Front, +
10. Defense II (85-7) Inside
11. Passing I (82-2) Technique+
12. Passing II (83-0) Cutting, Faking+, Communication
13. Rebounding/Picking (91-1)
14. The Transition Game (86-5)
15. Team Offense (87-3) Plays+
16. Team Defense (88-1) Help, Zones+
17. Full Court Pressure (89-X) Offense & Defense

Book & Video Discounts

Check our website or call for current discounts; some as high as 50-75%
▪9 book Series (02-4) ~**$20 off**, $78.00
▪2 book Bible Set (20-2) ~**$5 off**, $39.95
▪7 Guide Set (22-9) ~**$5 off**, $46.95
▪**$10 Off** Video 1 with Bible purchase
▪**$15 Off** Videos 2-4, $59.95
▪**$20 Off** Videos 1-4, $79.95

Clinics (2000,2001)- Check for current

Five different clinics: **Right Stuff(coaches);
Everything -2 days; Shooting; Defense; Offense.**
Limited numbers!!!
For coaches/players (12min age) at all levels.
At Haverford College near Philly.
Payment secures place. Lodging available for as little as $15 night.

Clinic Schedule in Brief:

Start 9:30. Two hours of instruction. Lunch. Two additional hours of instruction. End 3:30. Check our website or call for current charges.

Cost per day:

Check our website for current prices
DATES:
Oct 15,00 + Oct 14,01 **Right Stuff**
June 23-24,2001 **Everything(2 day)**
July 7-8,2001 **Shooting-Defense**
July 21-22,2001 **Shooting-Offense**
Aug. 4-5,2001 **Defense-Offense**
Call 800-979-8642 or visit our website for more details.

HOW TO ORDER

Call 800-979-8642, Fax 215-438-5349 or use our web site:
www.mrbasketball.net
Use a credit card, PO (organizations only), check (we hold checks for 10 days) or money order.
Our address:
Golden Aura Publishing, P.O. Box 41012 Phila., PA 19127-1012

SHIPPING CHARGES (Check for current)

$25 Order–> $5 Shipping
▪add 75¢ shipping for each addn'l $25 of order
▪Add 7% sales tax for PA orders
▪Add $2 for shipments to a home

Supply this information with each order:
Your Name; Shipping Org if any; Street Address; City; State; Zip; home phone; work phone
Additional for Foreign Orders: **Province; Country**